Contents

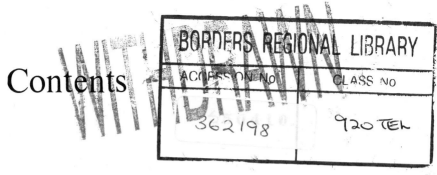

ACKNOWLEDGEMENTS

The author and publishers wish to thank the following for permission to reproduce the illustrations on the pages indicated: R. Hitchings, Crewe and Alsager College of Education, for the map of Telford's Canals on page 11; Mr Tom Boyd of Langholm for the medallion on the cover, 4; W. G. Cross and Sons, Shrewsbury 7; Aerofilms Ltd 15; Eileen Preston 35; The National Portrait Gallery 38. The author's thanks are due to the Staff of the Shropshire Record Office, Shrewsbury Borough Library and Manchester Central Reference Library for their assistance.

The cover photograph by Cadbury Lamb is of the Pontcysyllte aqueduct, 1805.

Printed in Great Britain by C. I. Thomas & Sons (Haverfordwest) Ltd, Press Buildings, Merlins Bridge, Haverfordwest.

Opposite: An engraving from the portrait of Thomas Telford by Samuel Lane, painted in 1822 for the Institute of Civil Engineers of which Telford was first President.

D0416399

Above: The village of Glendinning today, where Telford was born.

In Memory of
John Telford who after
living thirty three Years as
an unblameable shepherd
died at Glendining 12 Nov
1757 his son Thomas who
died an Infant.

Left: the headstone carved by Telford in memory of his father, now in Westerkirk parish churchyard.

Lifelines 10

Thomas Telford

An illustrated life of Thomas Telford

1757-1834

Rhoda M. Pearce

Shire Publications Ltd.

From stonemason to civil engineer

EARLY LIFE IN SCOTLAND

'I ever recollect with pride and pleasure my native parish of Westerkirk where I was born on the banks of the Esk in the year 1757. . .' To Thomas Telford the village of Glendinning in the parish of Westerkirk, Dumfriesshire, always remained home, and he returned there as often as possible to see his mother and friends.

He wrote often to the people he remembered there and these letters give some of the best glimpses of his working life. Particularly interesting are those he wrote to Andrew Little who attended the local parish school at Westerkirk with him and who later became the schoolmaster himself.

When Telford left school he was apprenticed to a stonemason, first at Lochmaben where he was very unhappy, and then at Langholm. He progressed from working on the simple stone walls in this mainly pastoral area to rebuilding houses for the estate workers. He eventually became a journeyman stonemason and constructed the bridge across the Esk at Langholm. When work was slack he engraved gravestones and ornamental doorheads and his first known work was the carving of a simple headstone in memory of his father who died three months before he was born.

By 1780 he had begun to find this employment limiting and he went to Edinburgh to study a wide range of works, particularly buildings like Holyrood House. So began his interest in architecture, closely linked to his practical craftsmanship in building. In 1782, at the age of 25, he travelled on horseback to London to widen his knowledge still further, and hopefully to make a career for himself as an architect and planner.

'In the year 1782 after having acquired the rudiments of my profession, I considered that my native country afforded few

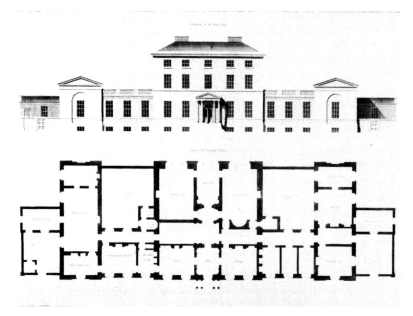

Telford's plan of the Commissioner's House at Portsmouth Dockyard.

opportunities of exercising it to any extent, and therefore judged it advisable (like many of my countrymen) to proceed southward, where industry might find more employment and be better rewarded.'

FIRST COMMISSIONS

Telford carried a letter of introduction from a Mrs Pasley of Langholm to her brother, a merchant in London. He was able to put Telford in touch with two great architects, Sir William Chambers and Robert Adam, who were working on the new Somerset House. Telford himself was employed on the project for two years and he 'acquired much practical information, both in the useful and ornamental branches of architecture'.

Having worked his way quickly into a career in architecture Telford was invited in 1784 to build a house at Portsmouth Dockyard for the resident commissioner. During his three years at Portsmouth he studied the dockyard itself, and this knowledge was to be very useful later, when he undertook dock and harbour projects in Wales and Scotland, culminating in the building of St. Katherine's Docks, London.

In 1787 this was far away and the immediate future held plans of a very different kind. For Telford was invited by Sir William Pulteney, M.P. for Shrewsbury and originally from Telford's own parish in Scotland, to make improvements to Shrewsbury Castle so that he could live in it while on business in the town. As a sequel to this assignment Telford was to undertake many varied works in Shropshire, moving out of the sphere of architecture into civil engineering.

While the repairs to Shrewsbury Castle were being carried out under Telford's direction, the magistrates were considering plans for a new prison. John Howard, the prison reformer, had studied the plans and felt that the cells were too small and the outside wall too close. He asked Telford to put his case to the magistrates, who allowed him to draw up new plans. The prison is still in use and the front entrance particularly has been little altered from Telford's original design.

The entrance to Shrewsbury Prison, designed by Telford. The bust is of John Howard, the prison reformer, who was instrumental in getting Telford the commission.

Telford's work became more and more diverse and included the excavation of the Romano-British town of *Uriconium,* near Shrewsbury, and the planning of a new county hospital. This was to become the Royal Salop Infirmary (now converted into flats and shops). He had less success in trying to persuade the churchwardens of St Chad's church to undertake major repairs to the walls and foundations. His prediction, that unless this was done the church would fall down proved to be true when soon afterwards the tower collapsed. Telford did not plan the new St Chad's, which was the work of George Steuart, but he was interested in church architecture and later planned the octagonal church of St Michael's, Madeley (now in Telford New Town), and St Mary's, Bridgnorth, the main part of which is almost square.

It was while working on these projects that Telford was 'employed as the surveyor of an extensive county'. Parts of Shropshire were intersected by the river Severn and its tributaries, and Telford's first task was to rebuild a number of bridges in strategic positions across the river. This was the real beginning of his civil engineering career which was soon to include so much more than just bridge building.

The first bridge he built was at a place called Montford Bridge where the Holyhead Road from Shrewsbury crossed the river Severn. The river channel was deep and narrow. It was also subject to high floods and therefore it was difficult to secure the foundations. To overcome this, piles were sunk into the banks, filled with earth. These supported a timber platform on which the bridge piers were built. The bridge itself had three arches and was built of local red sandstone. The bridge has since been rebuilt to take heavy holiday traffic on what is now the A5 to North Wales.

The bridge at Buildwas was to be a very different proposition. A short distance along the river the first iron bridge in Britain had been completed in 1779. Telford decided to build the bridge at Buildwas also of cast iron with a 130-foot span. The iron, like that at Ironbridge, was cast by the Coalbrookdale Company, but Telford's design was more graceful.

THE ELLESMERE CANAL

As Telford himself said, 'the time was now arrived when my professional pursuits were to be in a great measure changed.' He

*Left: St. Mary's
Bridgnorth,
Shropshire.*

*Below: the cast
iron bridge at
Buildwas,
Shropshire.*

must have watched with great interest the growing importance
of the early canals, and he noted that they 'had made
considerable progress in various parts of the Kingdom, and had
been particularly adopted in Shropshire.' In 1793 an Act of
Parliament allowed the Ellesmere Canal Company to construct a
network of canals to link the rivers Mersey, Dee and Severn.

Originally there were to be four main sections, from
Ellesmere Port on the Mersey (named for the termination of the
canal) to Chester; from Chester to the North Wales border with
a feeder from Llantysilio on the Dee; through the middle of
Shropshire to Shrewsbury; and a branch from this to join the
Montgomeryshire canal. The survey had been made by William
Jessop but, at an early meeting of the company Telford was
asked to be the chief engineer. 'I did not hesitate to accept their
offer, and from that time directed my attention solely to Civil
Engineering . . . ' In the early years of the canal project Telford
worked with Jessop and others, although, alas, not always
harmoniously.

The first section from Ellesmere Port presented no real
difficulties and at Chester it linked up with the old Chester to
Nantwich canal. Although only completed in 1779 this had
already become derelict because it had no links with other
waterways. Telford had to restore it, often rebuilding locks,
perhaps the most important being the ones he constructed near
Beeston, which were the first ever to be made of iron.

The middle section from Chester through North Wales proved
impossible to build because of the hilly land, mine workings and
lack of water supply, and had to be abandoned. Instead, Telford
constructed the Horseshoe Falls on the river Dee at Llantysilio
and guided the build-up of water into the canal which ran to
Pontcysyllte. To ensure a regular supply, Lake Bala, from which
the Dee flowed, was kept at a certain level from the end of the
winter by a regulating weir.

At Pontcysyllte, Telford was faced with the major
engineering problem of carrying the canal over the wide Dee
valley. He decided to construct an aqueduct which was raised
127 feet above the river and had to be carried by 18 stone piers
embedded firmly in sandstone rock. The water was carried in a
cast iron trough, 11 feet 10 inches wide, of which the tow-path
covered 4 feet 8 inches. The prototype for this undertaking was
almost certainly the aqueduct carrying the Shrewsbury Canal

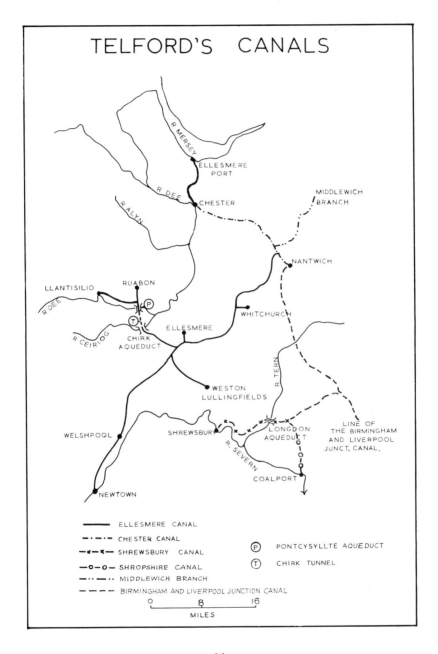

TELFORD'S CANALS

——————— ELLESMERE CANAL
—·—·— CHESTER CANAL
—x—x— SHREWSBURY CANAL
—o—o— SHROPSHIRE CANAL
—··—··— MIDDLEWICH BRANCH
— — — — BIRMINGHAM AND LIVERPOOL JUNCTION CANAL

Ⓟ PONTCYSYLLTE AQUEDUCT
Ⓣ CHIRK TUNNEL

0   8   16
MILES

over the river Tern (a tributary of the Severn) at Longdon. This was the first aqueduct to be built of cast iron plates bolted together.

The Pontcysyllte aqueduct was completed in 1805 and the opening ceremony was colourful and impressive.

'On the signal being given, the cannon on the western bank of the Dee. . . fired a royal salute . . The evening was calm and the favourite airs of "God Save the King" and "Rule Britannia" floated in the air amongst the echoes of the vale. Many (probably more than eight thousand people) were stationed all around us, from the tops of the mountains to the banks of the Dee, and were cheering and exulting, with intervals of silent astonishment.' [1]

From an engineering point of view the aqueduct has never been surpassed and is still one of the 'wonders of Wales'. There is little doubt that it was Telford's achievement, but he was helped by very able men, especially by Matthew Davidson as superintendent, who had worked with him on Montford Bridge and was to conduct operations on the eastern end of the Caledonian Canal.

By 1805 the last section of the canal had been completed through the Shropshire and Cheshire countryside. It had been decided to link up with the Chester to Nantwich canal at Hurleston which would provide an outlet for the traffic coming from North Wales. The branch to Shrewsbury was never completed but the Montgomeryshire section took it almost to Newtown. Telford continued to inspect the canal works regularly but with the completion of the actual construction he returned to Scotland 'where political circumstances occurred which led to my connection with a work of unusual magnitude'.

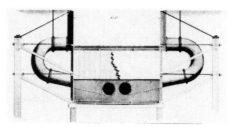

Telford's plan of the transverse section of one of the cast iron locks on the Ellesmere Canal.

The Caledonian and Gotha canals

BUILDING THE CALEDONIAN CANAL

'The work of unusual magnitude' which was to engage so much of Telford's time and energy for the next twenty years was the Caledonian Canal in Scotland. The valley of the Great Glen was made by a series of rivers which widened into natural lochs linking the Atlantic with the North Sea. All but twenty miles of its length was already navigable. In 1773 James Watt had been asked to survey the possible route of a canal to link the lochs, and his report was favourable.

These plans were shelved until 1801 when the war with France adversely affected trade and caused the diversion of ships around the north of Scotland. This passage was hazardous anyway, and it was felt that an inland waterway would get around the difficulties, as well as providing work for some of the many unemployed in the Highlands. In that year the government appointed two boards of commissioners, one for making roads and bridges to open up the Highlands, and the other for building the Caledonian Canal. Telford became surveyor and then chief engineer to both. The secretary to the Commissioners, John Rickman, worked very closely with Telford. They remained friends right up to his death, and it was Rickman who persuaded him to write his autobiography and eventually edited it.

The building of the canal raised many engineering difficulties which Telford had not envisaged. It was not completed until 1822 and even then it was unsatisfactory because ships had increased in size and speed. In 1847 it had to be deepened and virtually restored.

The canal ran from near Inverness to Loch Eil (near Fort William), and the work started from both ends, eventually meeting at the highest level. At the eastern end near Inverness, the entrance from the Moray Firth to the canal was by a tidal lock, 170 feet long and 40 feet wide. From this an embankment was built across the shore to another lock of the same size at Clachnacharry. To the south of this was a large basin 967 yards long and 162 yards wide. Four locks lifted the canal 32 feet out of the basin on to a level with Loch Ness. The canal actually used the bed of the river until it passed through a regulating lock into Loch Dochfor which runs into Loch Ness. Loch Ness is 22 miles long, at least a mile wide and very deep. By June 1818 this part of the work had been completed and ships were able to pass from the Moray Firth to Fort Augustus on Loch Ness. Matthew Davidson had been in charge of this very difficult stage from the beginning, with John Cargill as contractor. Davidson lived just long enough to see it completed. He was a tough character who had worked on Telford's greatest projects but who had particularly loved the area around Pontcysyllte. He had brought many of the Welsh workers from there, both skilled and unskilled, to work on the Caledonian Canal. Most of the locks and bridges were built of cast iron imported from Derbyshire and Wales. Davidson was succeeded by his youngest son, James.

Fort Augustus became the headquarters of James Davidson's team and from there they constructed a flight of locks to take the canal down to the level of the river Oich and then alongside

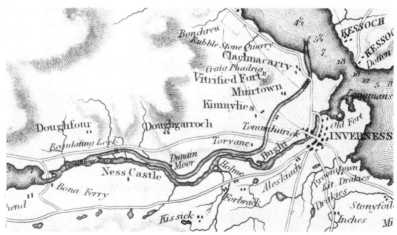

Telford's map of the eastern end of the Caledonian Canal, showing the tidal lock at the Moray Firth entrance.

The central part of the Caledonian Canal passing through the Great Glen.
The whole project took eleven years longer than forecast and required
rebuilding in the 1840s to meet the changed needs of sea-going craft.

the river to Loch Oich. On this stretch there was the Kytra
Lock and a regulating lock

At the western end of the canal John Telford (no relation)
was in charge of the operations until 1807 when he died and
Alexander Easton took over. Again a great sea lock was built at
Corpach, this time out of rock. The canal entered a basin and
then, after a mile, was carried up a flight of eight locks at
Benavie, which became known as Neptune's Staircase. Robert
Southey, the poet, accompanied Telford on one of his
inspection tours and in his journal wrote as follows, 'When we
drew near enough to see persons walking over the lock-gates, it
had more the effect of a scene in a pantomime than of anything
in real life. The rise from lock to lock is eight feet, 64 therefore
in all; the length of the locks, including the gates and abutments

at both ends, 500 yards—the greatest piece of such masonry in the world, and the greatest work of its kind, beyond all comparison.' ²

Between the staircase and Loch Lochy an aqueduct of three arches carried the canal across the river Loy. In this section, especially, the canal could easily overflow because of the water coming down from the mountains and therefore sluices and culverts were built to regulate the level. After the completion of this section the 'western men', under John Wilson their contractor, joined Cargill and Davidson at Fort Augustus.

The remaining work for the western team was a regulating lock taking the canal into Loch Lochy with two locks to take it out. Finally, the canal passed through the Laggan cutting into Loch Oich which had to be deepened by rather laborious methods—steam dredgers and horse-drawn carts carrying away the earth.

'We walked along the works between the Lakes Oich and Lochy. Here the excavators are what they call "at deep cutting", this being the highest ground on the line, the Oich flowing to the East, the Lochy to the Western Sea. This part is performed under contract by Mr. Wilson, a Cumberland man from Dalston, under the superintendance of Mr. Easton, the resident Engineer.'

This central section of the canal was to test Telford's engineering skill to the utmost as well as the resources of his contractors, and took very much longer than expected. In the end, parts of it had to be hurried, a disastrous policy leading later to the closing of the canal until the 1840s, when it was rebuilt.

The whole project was very much criticised in Parliament and in public. It had taken eighteen years instead of the seven Telford had predicted, and the cost was over £980,000, very much more than forecast. There was always a shortage of money and John Telford, particularly, often had difficulty paying his men. Telford himself had problems with the Parliamentary Commissioners, especially when he did not obey their instructions.

Above all, many of the reasons for building the canal had disappeared by the time it was finished: the war with France had ended, many ships were too large to get through the locks, and the fast steamships were more easily able to navigate the

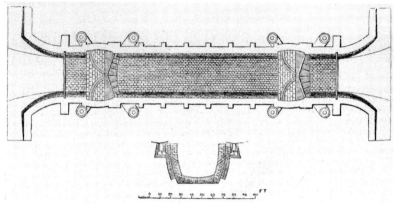

Plan of a lock on the Caledonian Canal.

northern sea route.

Despite all the criticisms Telford was able to say in his biography that 'this great and difficult work, performed in twenty years, in a remote district; and under a variety of other disadvantages, is proof of what may be accomplished by judicious arrangement and steady perseverance.'

VON PLATEN AND THE GOTHA CANAL

During the twenty years that Telford was working on the Caledonian Canal he was also advising on numerous other projects all over Britain and even further afield, in Sweden. Here Count Von Platen had watched Telford's canal work, particuarly, with great interest as he hoped to construct a waterway (the Gotha Canal) across Sweden, linking the North Sea and the Baltic. The western end had already been completed when Telford was invited to visit Sweden to survey the rest of the route, and he drew up plans for cutting 53 miles of new canal to link up the lakes.

Von Platen persuaded the Swedish government to back the project with financial aid and most of the building operations were carried out by soldiers and sailors. Unfortunately they had no engineering experience, so Von Platen brought over skilled British workers as well as examples of tools and plans of locks and bridges used in the Caledonian Canal.

Samuel Bagge became the resident engineer and Telford had little practical contact with the work, as he was only able to

17

visit Sweden twice. On the second occasion he advised that the policy of sporadic work all along the canal should cease and that the contractors should concentrate on certain sections between locks so that they could be opened and used by traffic. He arranged for eight more engineers, mainly Scots, to join the team. This proved particularly necessary after Bagge's sudden death but they did not find it easy working on such a difficult project in a foreign country and there was a good deal of high-handedness and quarrelling between them and the Swedish workers.

Like the Caledonian Canal the Gotha took much longer to complete, cost more money and encountered greater engineering problems than had been envisaged. There was a good deal of opposition to it and Von Platen himself took charge of the most difficult part, that of deepening a passage through Lake Viken which led into the largest lake, Vattern. The bottom of the lake was made up of jagged rocks and these had to be exposed and blasted out. The work was completed by bringing the most skilled workers to the site while the rest of the work on the canal had halted for the winter.

Von Platen did not live to see the work completed in 1832 for he had died three years earlier. Like the Caledonian Canal the Gotha never achieved the success hoped for, although it is still used by passenger traffic. Von Platen must be given the credit for the promotion and eventual completion of the canal, but he relied a great deal on Telford's plans and advice and there are similarities between the locks and bridges on the Gotha and those on Telford's canals in Britain. They remained close friends and the continuous correspondence which was carried on between the two gives insight into Telford's warm and friendly personality.

Highland roads and bridges

COMMUNICATIONS IN THE HIGHLANDS

While Telford was advising on these 'works of unusual magnitude' he was also engaged on rather more mundane, but also more extensive, work on roads and bridges in the Highlands. He made his first report on the situation to the Parliamentary Commissioners in 1802 and went on reporting on the progress made for a further twenty eight years. Initially he had been asked to find out the reasons for the increasing emigration from the Highlands. He felt that the main reason was the starvation of the land and the consequent change over to sheep farming. He recommended improvement in communications as a first step to economic development. The problems and scale of the work were immense, for the only existing communications were tracks, or roads built for military purposes.

Telford was made responsible for all new roads and for repairing existing ones. The civil roads in the Highlands were a very different proposition from those in the Lowlands, as the countryside was mountainous and rugged and the tracks were therefore narrow with steep inclines. Increasing demands were being put on these, especially by the growing numbers of Highland cattle being driven south into England to be fattened up and sold for meat. This kind of traffic required a relatively smooth road surface and had to be taken into consideration in road construction.

After 1802 the landowners could apply to the Parliamentary Commissioners if they felt that a road for public and private use was needed in their area. Telford was then asked to survey the proposed route and to report to the Commissioners, giving an estimate of how much the work would cost. If this was approved then the petitioners had to deposit half the estimated cost with the Bank of Scotland, the other half being met by the

Commissioners on the government's behalf.

Telford then prepared detailed working drawings and specifications and marked out the precise line on the ground. In the early years he carried out this work himself, partly because of the engineering difficulties and partly because he had more time. Later, when he was also surveying the Holyhead Road, he appointed a general surveyor over all the Highland road work. The first was John Duncombe, who had worked with him on the Ellesmere Canal. He proved hopelessly inadequate and after five years of frustration Telford appointed John Mitchell, a tough, energetic stonemason who travelled hundreds of miles each year inspecting the work. After 1814, Mitchell also took over the repair of military roads, then controlled by the Commissioners. Telford was able to rely on him completely until Mitchell's sudden death in 1824, when he was succeeded by his rather less successful son, Joseph.

Careful organisation went into the building of each road. One of the superintendents who had helped with the original survey was put in charge of the operation and he showed the plans to the contractors. If the road was more than ten miles long, the work was split up among a number of firms. These were appointed after sending their tenders to the Commissioners. On acceptance of a tender a contract was signed and the work progressed under the superintendent and a special inspector appointed by Telford. The latter made a monthly statement on the progress of the work to the Commissioners and in this way contractors were kept strictly to the agreed specifications. Telford himself said that 120 separate contracts were successfully carried out, and there is no doubt that a number of respected contracting firms were established in Scotland as a result of this work.

The problems involved in building roads in mountainous country were immense. Getting raw materials, such as lime for mortar and arch stones for bridges, was a long and difficult operation. They were brought as far as possible by sea and then overland by packhorse. For the foundation and surface of the road, local stone was used, but even this often had to be carried over difficult country.

Getting and keeping workers was also a problem although there were, of course, still a large number of unemployed in the Highlands. At first the men lived in temporary huts but this was

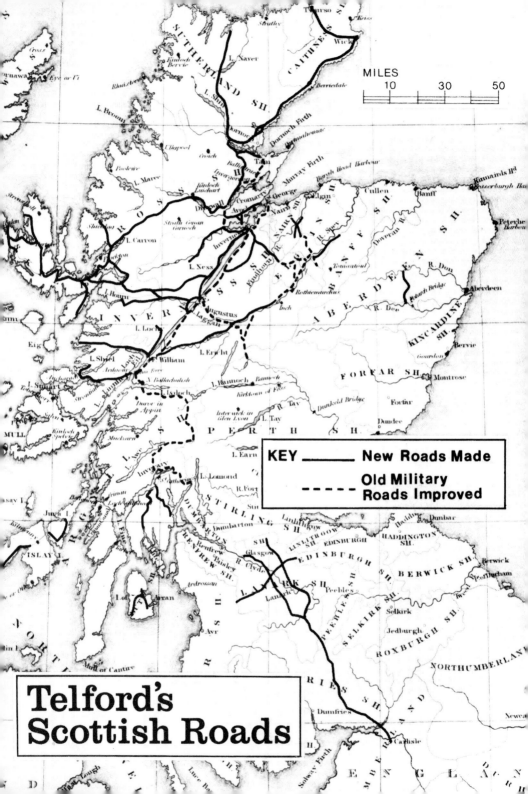

Telford's Scottish Roads

expensive and time-consuming when the building operations were always on the move. The huts were therefore replaced by military canvas tents, although they were not liked by the men themselves. Eventually in 1824, when more roads were able to take wheeled vehicles, large caravans were introduced which were reasonably comfortable as well as being mobile.

ECONOMIC EFFECTS OF THE NEW ROADS

The work of Telford and his associate engineers in building a network of roads through the Highlands is usually overshadowed by his other engineering marvels, such as the Pontcysyllte aqueduct and the Menai Bridge. However, there is no doubt that from the social, economic and engineering point of view, the achievement and the effects of this road-building project were considerable.

There was no exaggeration in Joseph Mitchell's letter (recorded in Telford's autobiography), which said:

'Since that period (before 1803), the progress of these works has gradually laid open the most inaccessible parts of the country; and the Commissioners, by combining the efforts of all the counties in the prosecution of one great general measure of improvement, have succeeded in effecting a change in the state of the Highlands, perhaps unparalleled in the same space of time in the history of any country.'

Mitchell went on to record in detail the results of the improvements. Coaching services were established along the main roads and inns were built at regular stages to cater for passengers. Letters and newspapers could be carried much more quickly and many places had their first regular post. Trade increased as goods were conveyed more easily by regular carriers, and the roads were linked to the Caledonian Canal and to the harbours improved or built by Telford on the coast.

The building of the 'Commissioners' roads' had a snowball effect in encouraging the building of 'district' roads to link up with them, so that landowners and crofters were able to use carts instead of packhorses for carrying goods. Cottages could now be improved as materials were brought in more easily. The value of land and property increased as areas became more accessible. It was this effect which was to be most important for the Highlands economically. Lime could be brought in to improve the soil, more advanced ploughs were used, and more

22

Above: a painting of Telford on a tour of inspection in 1820. Below: plans of road building, showing Telford's methods of constructing and improving roads to survive the Scottish climate.

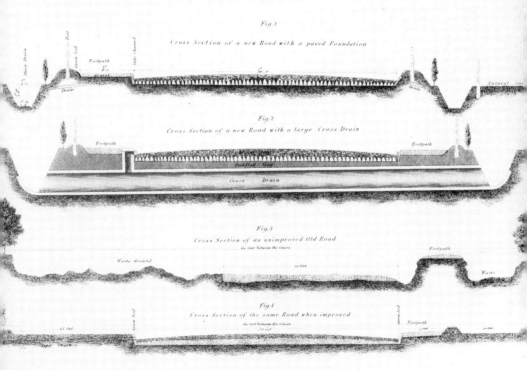

ROAD MAKING.

Fig. 1

Cross Section of a new Road with a paved Foundation

Fig. 2

Cross Section of a new Road with a large Cross Drain

Fig. 3

Cross Section of an unimproved Old Road

Fig. 4

Cross Section of the same Road when improved

Fig. 5

wheat was grown in areas like Ross and Sutherland and then exported to London. Mills were established for making flour. In many areas of the Highlands trees were planted which could later be cut down and the timber sold made a considerable contribution to the economy.

Alongside this an impetus was given to improvements in the breeding of animals, as Cheviot sheep, Ayrshire cattle and draft horses were brought in. This affected both the small and the large farmer and as a result their crofts were improved. This was confirmed in a letter from a gentleman in Sutherland who said that the improved roads affected the whole attitude of the people, because they felt less cut off. Financially the improvements were reflected in the establishment of banks in what had been an undeveloped area.

BRIDGES IN THE LOWLANDS

Telford completed the communications network by improving roads in the Lowlands of Scotland, the most important being that between Glasgow and Carlisle. He also worked on many bridges, ranging from small single-span structures over streams and waterfalls to complicated ones over wide and deep rivers. Some were built of iron and some of stone. It is impossible to go into detail on these but different types are illustrated, and one description by Southey of the Craig-Elachie bridge will serve as an example of the great skill employed. It also shows that Telford was careful to blend the structure into the background, and most of his bridges in Scotland are beautiful as well as useful.

'It began to rain when we renewed our journey, but held up before we had advanced two miles when we came upon Craig-Elachie Bridge, one of Telford's works, and a noble work it is. The situation is very fine, under the crag from which it takes its name and of which a great part, to the height perhaps of 100 feet has been cut away in making the road to it. The road brings the traveller by a short tour to the two short turrets at the entrance of the bridge. On this side they are merely ornamental, on the other their weight is necessary for the abutment. The bridge is of iron, beautifully light, in a situation where the utility of lightness is instantly perceived. The span is 150 feet, the rise 20 from the abutments, which are themselves 12 above the usual level of the stream. The only defect, and a

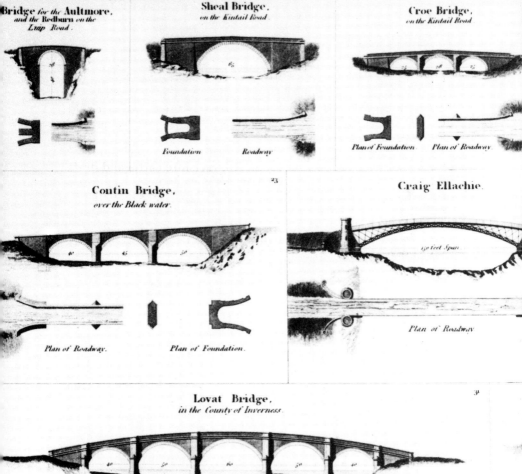

Bridge for the Aultmore,
and the Redburn on the
Lairg Road.

9, 10

Sheal Bridge,
on the Kintail Road.

11

Foundation Roadway

Croe Bridge,
on the Kintail Road

Plan of Foundation Plan of Roadway.

Contin Bridge,
over the Black water.

23

Plan of Roadway. Plan of Foundation.

Craig Ellachie.

150 feet Span.

Plan of Roadway.

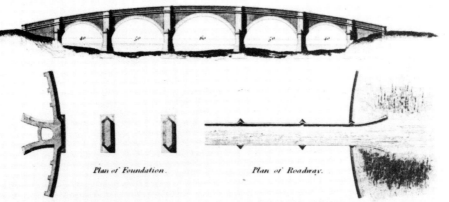

Lovat Bridge,
in the County of Inverness.

Plan of Foundation. Plan of Roadway.

These designs of bridges built by Telford in Scotland, are taken from a larger plan in 'The Atlas to the Life of Thomas Telford by Himself', edited by J. Rickman, 1838.

sad one it is, is that the railing for the sake of paltry economy is of the meanest possible form, and therefore altogether out of character with the rest of the iron work that being beautiful for its complexity and lightness. But this farthing-wisdom must now appear in everything that the Government undertakes; and thus the appearance of this fine bridge has been sacrificed for the sake of a saving, quite pityful in such a work. Mr. T. undertook to finish the bridge in twelve months: it was begun in June, and opened the October following. The iron work was cast at Plas Kynaston and brought by the canal over the great aqueduct at Pontey Syllty. The whole cost of the bridge and approaches on each side was £8,200.' [4]

A portrait of Robert Southey by T. Phillips, R.A. Southey greatly admired Telford and they became lasting friends.

The Holyhead Road

PRIVATE LIFE

From the time he arrived in London until 1810, Telford's life appeared to be filled with an increasing and almost impossible load of work. He travelled around all the time advising and inspecting, but he could not be everywhere at once and he therefore appointed assistants, a policy that aided the general development of civil engineering by training men to continue Telford's work.

We know little of Telford's private life except what we can glean from his letters to Andrew Little, his friend in Langholm, from the writing of Robert Southey and from the opinions of those who worked with him. He never married but appears to have had a large circle of friends ranging from those in government circles to the innkeepers and workers he met on his travels.

Even in the days at Portsmouth he filled most of his time with work, as is shown in the following letter he wrote to Andrew Little in 1786.

'You ask me what I shall do all winter. I rise in the morning at 7 o'clock and will continue to get up earlier until it comes to 5. I then set seriously to work, to make out Accounts, write on business, or draw till breakfast which is at 9. Going around amongst the several Works brings My dinner time, which is about 2 o'clock; an hour and a half serves this, at half after 3 I again make appearance when there's generally something wanted and I again go round and see what is going on—and draw till 5; then go to Tea till six—then I come back to my room and write, draw or read till half after 9—then comes Supper and Bed Time. This is my ordinary round unless when I dine or spend an Evening with a friend but friends of this sort I do not make many.' [5]

When working on the Caledonian Canal, Highland roads and

other projects, Telford must have spent much more of his day travelling, considering the distances and the slow rate of moving on horseback or by gig. One person who accompanied him on an inspection tour of Scotland was Robert Southey, who thought highly of him as a person and as an engineer. He met Telford for the first time in Edinburgh. 'Mr. Telford arrived in the afternoon from Glasgow, so the whole party were now collected. There is much intelligence in his countenance, so much frankness, kindness and hilarity about him flowing from the never-failing well-spring of a happy nature, that I was upon cordial terms with him in five minutes.'[6]

After the tour Southey was even more impressed and gives us one of the best glimpses of Telford's character.

'Here (Keswick) we left Mr. Telford, who takes the mail for Edinburgh. This parting company, after the thorough intimacy which a long journey produces between fellow travellers who like each other, is a melancholy thing. A man more heartily to be liked, more worthy to be esteemed and admired, I have never fallen in with; and therefore it is painful to think how little likely it is that I shall ever see much of him again—how certain that I shall never see so much. Yet I trust he will not forget his promise of one day making Keswick on his way to or from Scotland.'[7]

Southey comments on Telford's life and gives a useful description of Telford's road-building methods after watching his men at work. 'Telford's is a happy life: everywhere making roads, building bridges, forming canals and creating harbours—works of sure, solid, permanent utility; everywhere employing a great number of persons. The plan upon which he proceeds in road making is this: first to level and drain, then, like the Romans, to lay a solid pavement of large stones, the round or broad end downwards, as close as they can be set; the points are then broken to about the size of walnuts, laid over them, so that the whole are bound together; over all a little gravel if it be to hand, but this is not essential.'[8]

PARNELL AND THE HOLYHEAD ROAD

In fact, Telford's method of road-building varied according to the type of land the road was passing through, and this is seen clearly in the largest single project that he undertook, the London to Holyhead Road.

The road above Nant Ffrancon on the Holyhead Road.

He was brought into this partly because of his established reputation as a civil engineer but also because of his contact with members of Parliament. Sir Henry Parnell was an Irish member and therefore the journey from Ireland was particularly important to him. The road between Shrewsbury and Holyhead was slow and in some places hazardous. The poor state of this section was continually being raised in Parliament, and eventually a committee of the House of Commons was formed in May 1810. Telford was asked by the committee to make the surveys and on 22nd April 1811 he submitted a full report on how the work should be undertaken. The committee urged the making of detailed plans based on Telford's report but nothing was done to organise a practical scheme until Sir Henry Parnell secured the appointment of a Parliamentary Commission in 1815. They were to direct the necessary plans and estimates, and to administer the money granted by Parliament. Telford

Telford's plan of the Waterloo Bridge at Betws-y-Coed.

was appointed by them as engineer and it was his task 'to arrange, direct and superintend all practical operations'.

The road between London .and Shrewsbury remained under the control of the numerous turnpike trusts and the necessary improvement and maintenance was carried out by them. Nevertheless, Telford appointed one principal assistant to make annual reports to the Commissioners of what had been achieved and what needed to be done. As in Scotland, the practical work along the whole route was put out to contractors. Between Shrewsbury and Holyhead much of the road had to be rebuilt, and Telford advised, after the initial work had been undertaken, that the seven turnpike trusts should be amalgamated and taken over by the Commission. This was authorised by an Act of Parliament in 1819. To help him Telford appointed one principal assistant on the section, with four inspectors under him. In some cases the road was re-routed to make it shorter, as at Chirk; in others the gradient through mountainous country had to be modified, and bridges had to be constructed over steep river valleys. Most notable of these were the Waterloo Bridge over the river Conway at Betws-y-Coed, with its inscription commemorating the battle of Waterloo delicately wrought in the iron, and the bridge at Conway itself.

The Conway Bridge is well known today by holiday makers in North Wales, although it no longer carries road traffic across the Straits. It was a suspension bridge, to take the place of the ferry, and it was designed to blend with the castle architecture. The building of this bridge was very much overshadowed by that of the bridge over the Menai Straits but in many ways it was a greater achievement, as a long embankment had to be built approaching the bridge to cover the tidal waters of the Conway which carried a strong current. Conway was, in fact, off the main Shrewsbury to Holyhead route, but formed part of the older Chester Road which was still used by many travelling between Ireland and the North of England.

The most difficult engineering feat along the main route was to make a road with smooth gradients through Snowdonia, cutting through from the Waterloo Bridge at Betws-y-Coed and then towards Bangor, with the mountains on either side. In places the rock was blasted away to make a pass as at Nant Ffrancon, perhaps one of the outstanding examples of skilful engineering. Most picturesque is the passing of Lake Ogwen, done with such apparent ease. 'This road, established through a rugged and mountainous district, partly along the slope of rocky precipices, and across inlets of the sea, where the mail and other coaches are now enabled to travel at the rate of nine or ten miles an hour, was indeed an arduous undertaking, which occupied fifteen years of incessant exertion.' Today this is still the route of the A5, and the fact that it carries fast, heavy traffic without any great problems of gradient or bends is surely a tribute to Telford's genius.

THE MENAI STRAITS

However, for Telford, having reached Bangor, the most serious problem was still to be overcome—how to replace the slow and expensive ferry across the Menai Straits and how to cross the sands separating Holyhead itself from the rest of Anglesey. Telford decided to make, across the Stanley sands, an embankment 1,300 yards long and sixteen feet high This was opened in 1823 and saved the traveller a distance of about five miles.

The difficulties of crossing the Straits were immense. The tides ran in different directions, often advancing or retreating at considerable speed, and the Straits, in the vicinity of high mountains, often suffered strong winds and violent storms.

Telford's plan of the Conway Bridge.

Apart from these factors a passage had to be left open for the considerable amount of shipping which passed along the Straits.

After consultation with other engineers, and using his own experience in bridge building, Telford planned a suspension bridge based on his proposed bridge at Runcorn over the river Mersey (a bridge was not in fact built here until many years later). The roadway across the Menai Straits was suspended by sixteen great chains which were attached to two main stone piers on either side of the water. The one on the Anglesey side was built into a rock which remained above the water even at high tide. On the Caernarvon side the pier had to be carried under the water six feet to obtain a firm rock foundation Each of these piers was 153 feet above the high water level of the river. On the Anglesey side they were flanked by three smaller piers and archways which carried the road on to the land, and on the Caernarvon side by four smaller piers and archways. The resident engineer, William Provis, was a young man appointed by Telford because he felt he had a promising future. The stone work was contracted out to an experienced firm of masons, Straphen and Hall, and the iron work to William Hazeldine of

Shrewsbury who had done much of the iron work on the
Pontcysyllte aqueduct, the Waterloo and other bridges.
Straphen and Hall did not superintend their workers carefully
enough and the firm of John Wilson, at the time working on the
Gotha Canal, took over the masonry contract and completed it.

The roadway itself was a dual carriageway, each side being
twelve feet wide with a four foot path for pedestrians in
between them. It was along this road that the first vehicle, the

London mail-coach, passed, after the completion of the bridge
on 30th January 1826.

Telford wrote in his autobiography, 'Upon my report of the
state of the works, the Commissioners determined that the
passage over the bridge should be opened on the 30th January
1826. The weather, about that time, proved very stormy; and
previously to the opening day, Sir Henry Parnell and myself
examined the entire structure, and found all necessary
arrangements made. On Monday morning, at half-past one
o'clock, the London mail-coach, occupied by W. A. Provis, W.

*Above: the Menai Bridge shortly after its opening. Opposite: the Menai
Bridge today, still the only road link between Anglesey and the mainland.*

Hazeldine, the two junior Wilsons, Thomas Rhodes and the mail-coach superintendent, was the first that passed over the estuary, at the level of 100 feet above that tideway which heretofore has presented a decisive obstruction to travellers. The Chester Mail passed at half-past three o'clock, and Sir Henry Parnell, with myself drove repeatedly over; about nine o'clock, and during the whole day, was an uninterrupted succession of passing carriages, horsemen and pedestrians, who had assembled to witness and enjoy the novelty; and in the evening all the workmen were regaled with a joyous festival.'

The *Shrewsbury Chronicle* of Friday, 3rd February 1826, described the bridge as, 'This stupendous structure', and there is no doubt that it was regarded at the time as a tremendous achievement. Perhaps the best comment on its success is that it is still the only road link between the mainland and Anglesey.

Throughout this complicated undertaking Telford remained calm. He seems to have had a way with people which encouraged them to have confidence in him and to work against the odds. This is seen in all his projects but it is particularly true of the Holyhead Road, where Telford had to work alongside the turnpike trusts hoping that they would eventually take over the administration and maintenance of the road. He did all he could to make travelling as efficient as possible, planning new types of toll-houses, toll-gates and milestones, and suggesting patterns of organisation. Detailed plans of these are included in his autobiography, and in Sir Henry Parnell's *Treatise on Roads.* A number of the toll-houses still remain, perhaps the best known being at Llanfair P.G. on the Anglesey side of the Menai Bridge. Distances on the road are still recorded on the original milestones.

The building of roads in Scotland and Wales was certainly not Telford's only work of this nature. He undertook many other road projects, including those in the Worcester, Gloucester and Bristol areas, South Wales and the Lowlands of Scotland. His bridge building, too, covered a wide area, and because of his reputation in this field he was asked to judge a competition for a bridge crossing the Avon gorge at Bristol. Telford rejected the designs, including that of Brunel. He later submitted his own plan but this time his was passed over in favour of Brunel's. This was a great disappointment for Telford and perhaps showed that his greatest work in engineering was coming to an end.

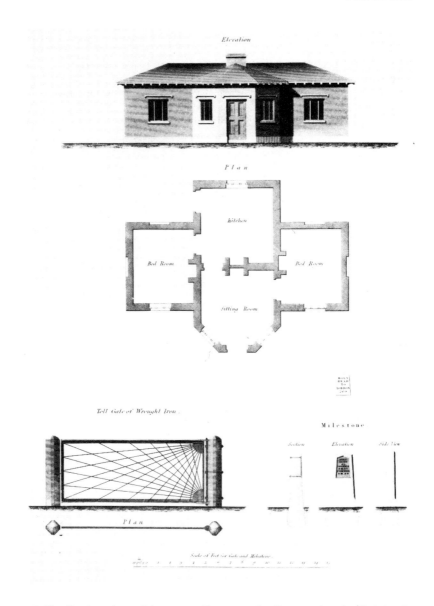

Telford's plans for toll-houses, toll-gates and milestones on the Holyhead Road.

11. G 34

Telford's last years

ST. KATHERINE'S DOCKS

By 1822, Telford had written to Von Platen, 'If you do not come this year or next there is a risk of the Game being over for us both. We play with so much eagerness—it cannot last long.'[9] In fact, he was to live and work for another twelve years but as he said, also to Von Platen, 'These great works being scattered over all England Scotland and Ireland require much more travelling than is consistent with comfort and, if I am not careful, with health.'[10]

It was in 1827, while on a tour of inspection of the Fens, that Telford contracted a chill resulting in a tendency to sickness which eventually killed him.

Nevertheless, in this last period of his life he was engaged in a large number of projects some of which were very significant. One of these was the building of St. Katherine's Docks, part of the great expansion of the London docks system, as near to the heart of the city as possible. Telford had already had experience in building the docks at Holyhead and along the Scottish coast but as engineer to the St. Katherine's Dock Company his skill was tested to the utmost in designing two docks on a very restricted site. (Two were necessary so that one could continue in use while the other was cleaned.)

Each dock of four acres was entered by 45 feet wide single lock gates from an entrance basin. This in turn was connected to the Thames by an entrance lock, 180 feet long and 45 feet wide with three pairs of gates. One large, or two small ships could pass through these at one time. The docks took only two and a half years to build and Telford felt there had been undue haste: '. . . I must be allowed to protest against such haste,

Opposite: a pencil drawing of Telford by William Brockenden, done three months before his death in 1834.

39

pregnant as it was, and ever will be, with risks, which, in more instances than one, severely taxed all my experience and skill, involving dangerously the reputation of directors and their engineers.'

WORK ON RAILWAYS

Telford himself had always been careful not to risk the lives of workmen and he felt that the new generation of directors were more concerned with speed and profit than with human lives. This was particularly true of some of the future railway engineers, and it was the effects of railway building that were to occupy much of Telford's later years in a number of different ways. It is difficult to judge his personal attitude to them because he was so much involved with the canal companies who opposed them. He says himself in connection with a survey of a route between Glasgow and Berwick in 1810 that, 'As most of the before mentioned obstacles objectionable to a canal are found in this proposed line of communications; it is evident a RAILWAY is here more advisable'.[11] The obstacles included passing through high ground, the difficulty of water supply, and frequent frost. In general he seems to have believed that canals were more efficient, especially for goods traffic, but that where they could not be built, the alternative should be a railway. He took considerable interest in railway projects and sent his assistants to study them. He did experiments comparing their efficiency in carrying goods with the canals. Using the Stockton and Darlington Railway as an example, he tried to show that rails and engines subject to heavy strain would wear out quickly, thereby incurring high costs of maintenance and repair. Although he certainly approved of steam traction he felt that its real future lay in steam carriages on the roads. Here he was partly wrong, for steam carriages never developed, but the roads *have* become the most economic means of carrying goods and passengers today.

Telford was closely involved in a curious way with the plans for the first really modern railway from Manchester to Liverpool. After the end of the Napoleonic Wars in 1815 there was a shortage of capital for all kinds of undertakings and consequently a high level of unemployment. To counteract this, in 1817 the Government set up an exchequer loan scheme which would make capital loans to deserving projects. Telford

The two Harecastle tunnels, showing Telford's new tunnel on the left and Brindley's original tunnel on the right. Telford was unable to persuade the company to improve the latter and it was later closed.

was appointed engineering adviser and he had to examine plans put forward by prospective borrowers. In many deserving cases he actually intervened and helped in planning, thus ensuring success, as in the Gloucester and Berkeley Canal.

Telford would much rather not have been involved in the Liverpool and Manchester Railway, as he knew there was considerable feeling against him as a canal builder. However, the planning of the railway had met with many difficulties and it was realised that the cost was going to be beyond the means of the company. They applied for an exchequer loan and Telford sent his assistant down to examine the scheme. The assistant was treated very badly, plans were withheld and Telford himself toured the route with George Stephenson in 1829. He was appalled at the sloppy organisation compared with his canal projects, where he used engineers for different stages of the route. Despite the bad feeling, his recommendations were adopted, the Liverpool and Manchester got its loan and was completed under more efficient organisation.

THE LAST CANAL

The canal companies were understandably worried by the threat of railway competition. Some of the earlier companies realised the need to improve their slow sections if they were to survive and this was particularly true of the Trent and Mersey, where boats were held up in passing through the many locks. Even more serious was the state of the Harecastle Tunnel, originally built by James Brindley. It had no tow-path and therefore involved 'legging' the boats through in single file. Telford was employed to draw up plans for a new tunnel with a tow-path. By working day and night, using steam engines to pump out the water continually, the project was finished in less than two years, being opened in 1827. It meant that boats passing in one direction could use the new tunnel, and in the other, Brindley's tunnel. Telford suggested to the company that the latter should be improved so that both could continue to be used safely. This was refused at the time because of the cost, but the company must have regretted their decision when later the old tunnel became so dangerous that it had to be closed.

The slowness of the Trent and Mersey in carrying traffic between Liverpool and the Midlands encouraged the idea of building a faster canal. The promoters of this later scheme had also been pushed into action by the threat of the formation of the Birmingham and Liverpool Junction Railway. Telford had already done considerable work to improve the Birmingham system of canals, especially by cutting a new canal between the city and Wolverhampton. The canal was wide, with a tow-path on each side, and used deep cuttings through the land, instead of locks and tunnels.

Before this work was completed the Birmingham and Liverpool Junction Canal Company was incorporated in 1826 with Telford as its chief engineer. The railway project was abandoned and the last important canal of the era was started. It was also the last victory of the canals over the railways and it was to be very short lived. In building it, Telford used his great engineering experience to make it as short and fast as possible. Instead of following the contours of the land, he cut through them using cuttings and embankments where necessary.

"In order to counteract the effects of the several railways which, about this time were proposed to be made between Liverpool and Birmingham, it became particularly desirable to carry the Birmingham and Liverpool Junction Canal in the shortest possible direction between the Birmingham Canal, near Wolverhampton, and the Ellesmere and Chester Canal at Nantwich, although this led to crossing the numerous inequalities of ground between the before-mentioned places, whereby this canal encountered cuttings and embankments of unusual magnitude, and proportionally expensive.'

There was also to be a branch from Norbury Junction on the main line to link with the Shrewsbury Canal, the first canal he had been involved with, so that coal and lime could be carried to Birmingham or London more easily.

Telford's last canal brought much opposition from landowners, partly because of increasing changes in farming and in the value of land, and meant that the ideal route had to be changed at considerable cost, involving greater engineering problems. This was especially true at Nantwich Basin, where the Birmingham and Liverpool Junction joined the Chester Canal. The ideal route planned by Telford ran from the basin through Dorfold Park. The owner of the estate objected so strongly that the canal had to be re-routed over a long curling embankment and aqueduct over the Chester road. The embankment does not look much today, compared with Telford's other achievements, but it caused great difficulties, as the heavy clay soil kept collapsing. Similarly, at Skelmore and Norbury the embankment did not hold and it was not until six months after Telford's death that the canal was opened to traffic.

It is significant that Telford used assistants here who had worked on his other projects. John Wilson was involved at Pontcysyllte, Alexander Easton on the Caledonian Canal and William Provis on the Holyhead Road. This was typical of Telford's attachment to the best of his assistants right up to his death.

INSTITUTION OF CIVIL ENGINEERS

He continued to inspect and report on the condition of his major works but increasingly he left on-site engineering to his assistants while he remained in his Abingdon Street home in London. Here he continued to entertain his friends and above all to advise and encourage young engineers. Many of them worked under him and he was particularly interested in their training and the exchange of ideas. He was determined to help

43

the advance of civil engineering as a profession and he was able to do this particularly when he became first president of the Institution of Civil Engineers. The position was a great honour which he fully appreciated and certainly deserved.

'Telford's position, both in public and in private life rendered him independent of favour or patronage; and he enjoyed the rare privilege of being his own master in the exercise of perfect impartiality, and of an undeviating adherence to what is abstractly just and proper; . . .'

The Institution had been started by a group of young engineers but it was Telford who really improved its status and position so that it was granted a Royal Charter in 1828. He organised the proceedings, initiated methods of recording them in the minutes and gradually built up a body of information on engineering practice. He encouraged research into different kinds of methods and materials, and he supplied the Institution with the nucleus of a lending library, on his death leaving it a valuable collection of books and documents. He was determined that the society was to be for the advance of civil engineering, a clearing house for experience so that all could benefit.

Telford continued to take an interest in all his projects right up to his death on 2nd September 1834. He was buried in Westminster Abbey.

His life is best summed up in his work which is an everlasting memorial to him, but if words are needed these can be taken from the obituary notice which appeared in the *Shrewsbury Chronicle.*

'His gradual rise from the stonemasons' and builders' yard to the top of his profession in his own country, or we believe we may say, in the world, is to be ascribed not more to his genius, his consummate ability and persevering industry, than to his plain honest, straightforward dealing and the integrity and candour which marked his character throughout life.'

Sources of quotations numbered in the text are as follows: 1 'Oration on the Opening of the Pontcysyllte Aqueduct from a Report of the Ellesmere Canal Company 1805'; 2, 3, 4, 6, 7 and 8 Robert Southey *Journal of a Tour of Scotland in 1819;* 5 and 11 Sir A. Gibb *The Story of Telford* 1935; 9 and 10 L.T.C. Rolt *Thomas Telford* 1952. Unnumbered quotations are from the *Life of Thomas Telford written by Himself,* edited J. Rickman.

THE PRINCIPAL EVENTS OF TELFORD'S LIFE

1757   Telford born at Glendinning, near Langholm, Dumfries
1760   *George III becomes king*
1761   *Duke of Bridgewater's Worsley-Manchester canal opened*
1769   *Watt's first steam engine*
1771   *Richard Trevithick born*
1780   Telford visits Edinburgh to study the buildings
1782   Telford goes to London where he works on Somerset House
1784   Telford begins work on the Commissioner's House at Portsmouth Dockyard
1787   Telford appointed as Surveyor of Public Works in Shropshire
1793   Work begins on the Ellesmere Canal. *War against France begins*
1801   Telford starts on plans for the Caledonian Canal. *Trevithick's Camborne road locomotive*
1802   Telford makes his first report to the Commissioners for Highland Roads and continues to report until 1830
1804   *Trevithick runs the first railway locomotive at Penydaren*
1805   Pontcysyllte Aqueduct and most of the Ellesmere Canal completed
1806   *Isambard Kingdom Brunel born*
1808   Telford makes survey on the Gotha Canal in Sweden
1815   Telford begins survey of the Holyhead Road. *French defeated at Waterloo*
1817   *Government Exchequer Loan Scheme*
1820   Telford first president of the Institution of Civil Engineers. *Accession of George IV*
1822   Work completed on the Caledonian Canal
1825   *Stockton to Darlington Railway opened*
1826   Menai Bridge opened and the 'new road' from London to Holyhead completed. Work starts on St. Katherine's Docks, London. Birmingham and Liverpool Junction Canal Company formed with Telford as chief engineer
1828   Work completed on St. Katherine's Docks
1830   *Liverpool and Manchester Railway opened. Accession of William IV*
1834   Telford dies and is buried in Westminster Abbey
1835   Birmingham and Liverpool Junction Canal opened.

SEEING TELFORD'S WORK

Memorials

A doorway made by Telford has been preserved in the grounds of Langholm Library (Dumfries, Scotland), to which he left £1,000.

A memorial tablet to him can be seen opposite the school and the library in Bentpath, Dumfries, Scotland. It was originally sited facing Glendinning on the Eskdalemuir road, near Bentpath, but was moved in 1979 because the site was dangerous.

His burial place is in Westminster Abbey.

Buildings in Shropshire
H.M. Prison, Shrewsbury
Shrewsbury Castle
St. Mary's Church, Bridgnorth
St. Michael's Church, Madeley, Telford.

Canals

The Ellesmere Canal, including the Horseshoe Falls at Llantysilio (near Llangollen, North Wales) and the magnificent Pontcysyllte and Chirk aqueducts, is one of the most attractive canals in Britain and carries an increasing number of holiday craft.

The Shrewsbury Canal, including the first iron aqueduct at Longdon, and the Shropshire Canal terminating with an inclined plane at Coalport are also of interest. The canals have become derelict but the route can still be followed and the Longdon aqueduct and the inclined plane have been preserved in situ by the Ironbridge Gorge Museum Trust.

The Birmingham and Liverpool Junction Canal remains very much as it was when Telford constructed it. In 1846 it was merged with the Ellesmere, Chester and Middlewich canals to form the Shropshire Union system. Since being taken over by British Waterways it has carried an increasing number of pleasure craft.

The Caledonian Canal, although improved, is very much as when Telford built it and, apart from the brilliant engineering, it passes through very beautiful scenery.

Roads and bridges

The A5 from London follows almost completely Telford's improved Holyhead Road, especially between Shrewsbury and

Anglesey. Some toll-houses and milestones can still be seen, as well as his Waterloo Bridge at Betws-y-Coed, and the Menai Bridge, both of which continue to carry traffic. Telford's Conway Bridge, designed to blend with the castle architecture, contrasts well with the modern road bridge which was built alongside it.

A living memorial
   Telford New Town in Shropshire was so named because it includes much of Telford's work within its boundaries—part of the Holyhead Road, part of the Shrewsbury and Shropshire canals and St. Michael's Church, Madeley.

BIBLIOGRAPHY
Life of Thomas Telford written by Himself; Edit. J. Rickman, 1838.

Journal of a Tour of Scotland in 1819; R. Southey; John Murray, 1929.

Lives of the Engineers, Vol.II (Telford and Rennie); S. Smiles; John Murray, 1874. Reprinted by David and Charles, 1968.

The Story of Telford; Sir A. Gibb; A. Maclehose & Co., 1935.

Thomas Telford; L.T.C. Rolt; Longman, 1958.

INDEX